This book belongs to

....

....

....

Illustrated by Vivi Markatos

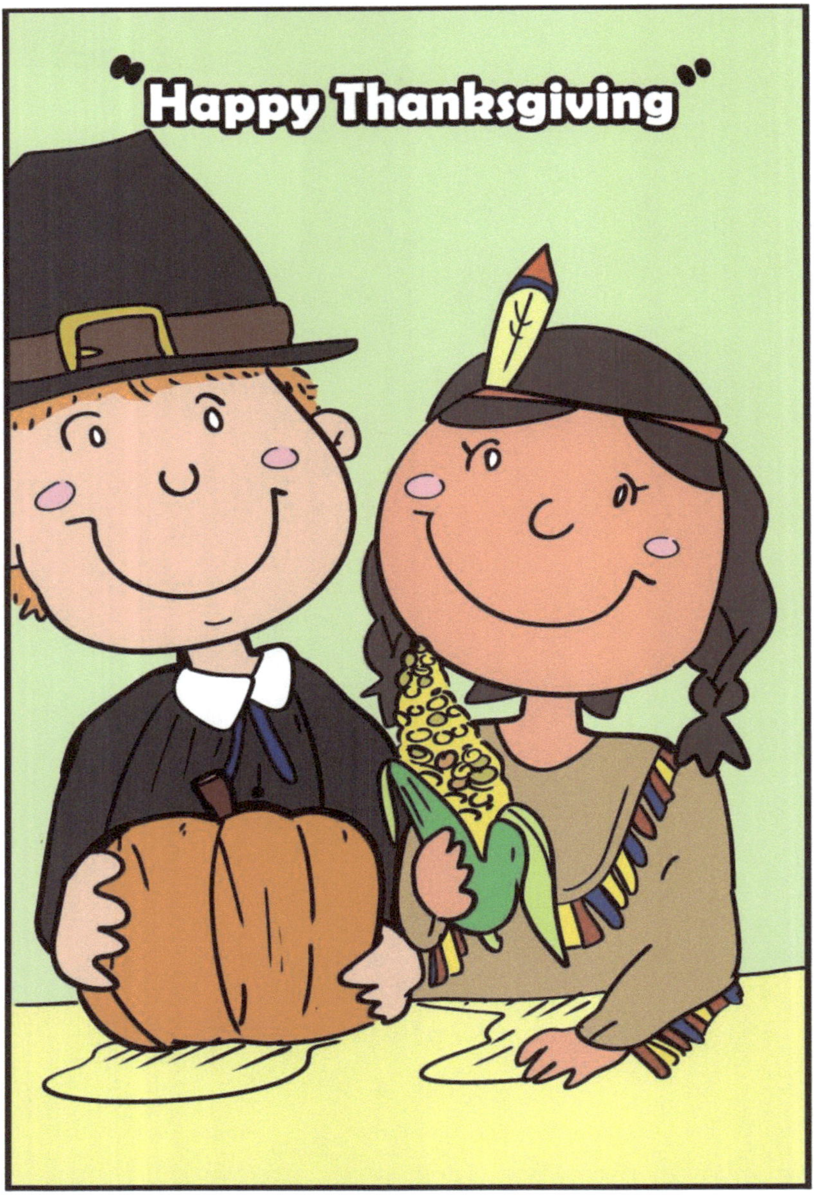
"Happy Thanksgiving"

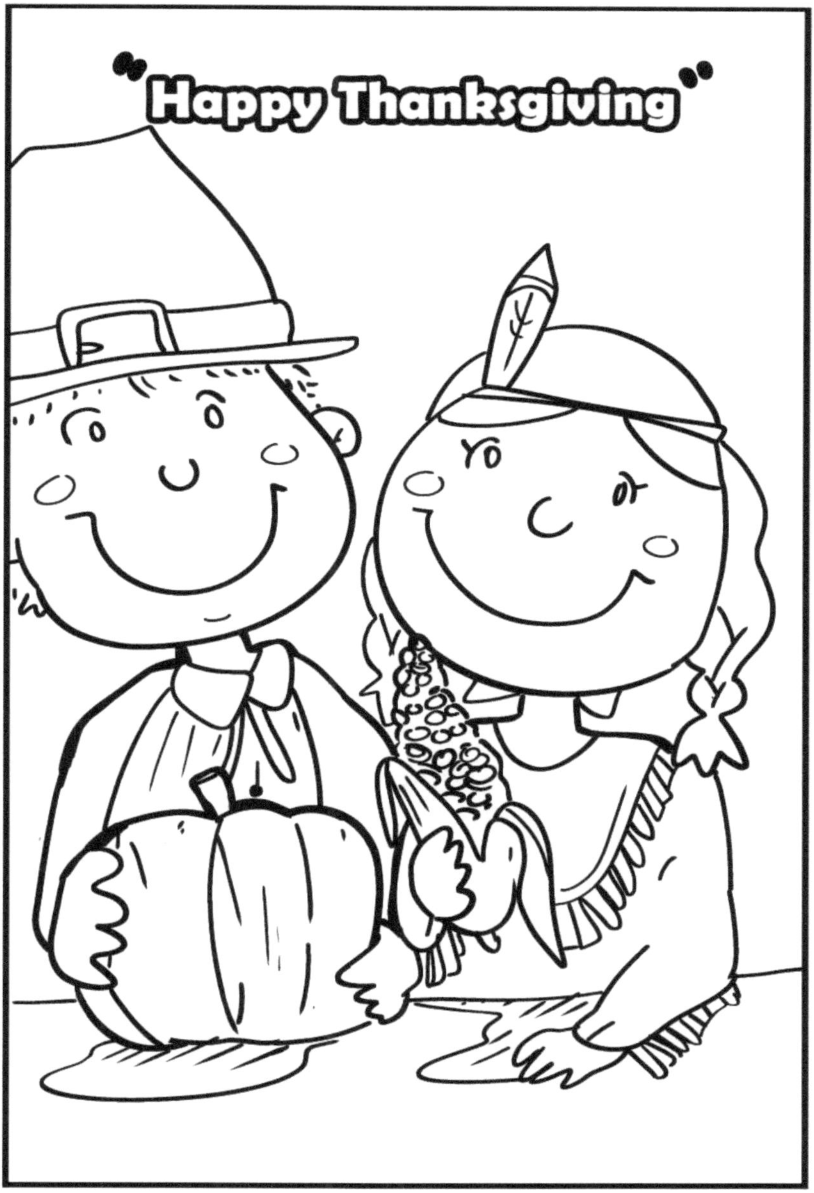
"Happy Thanksgiving"

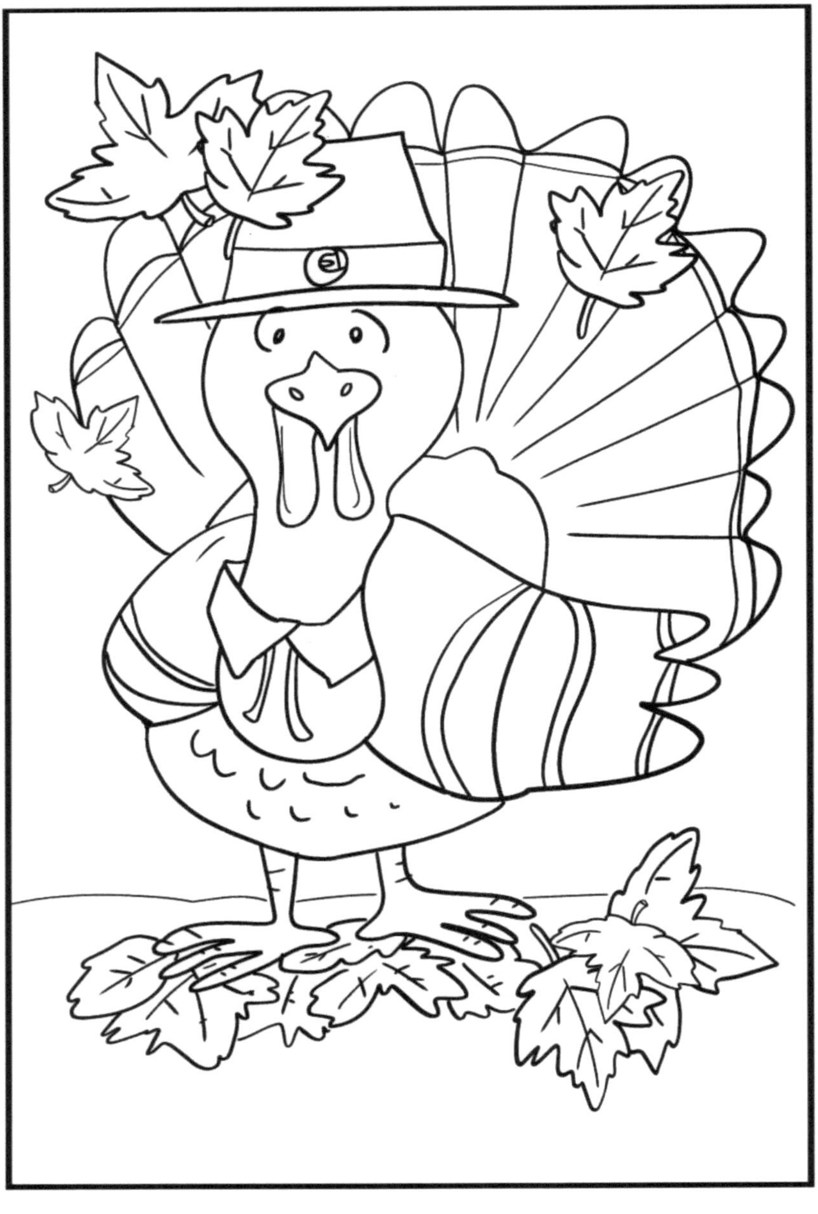

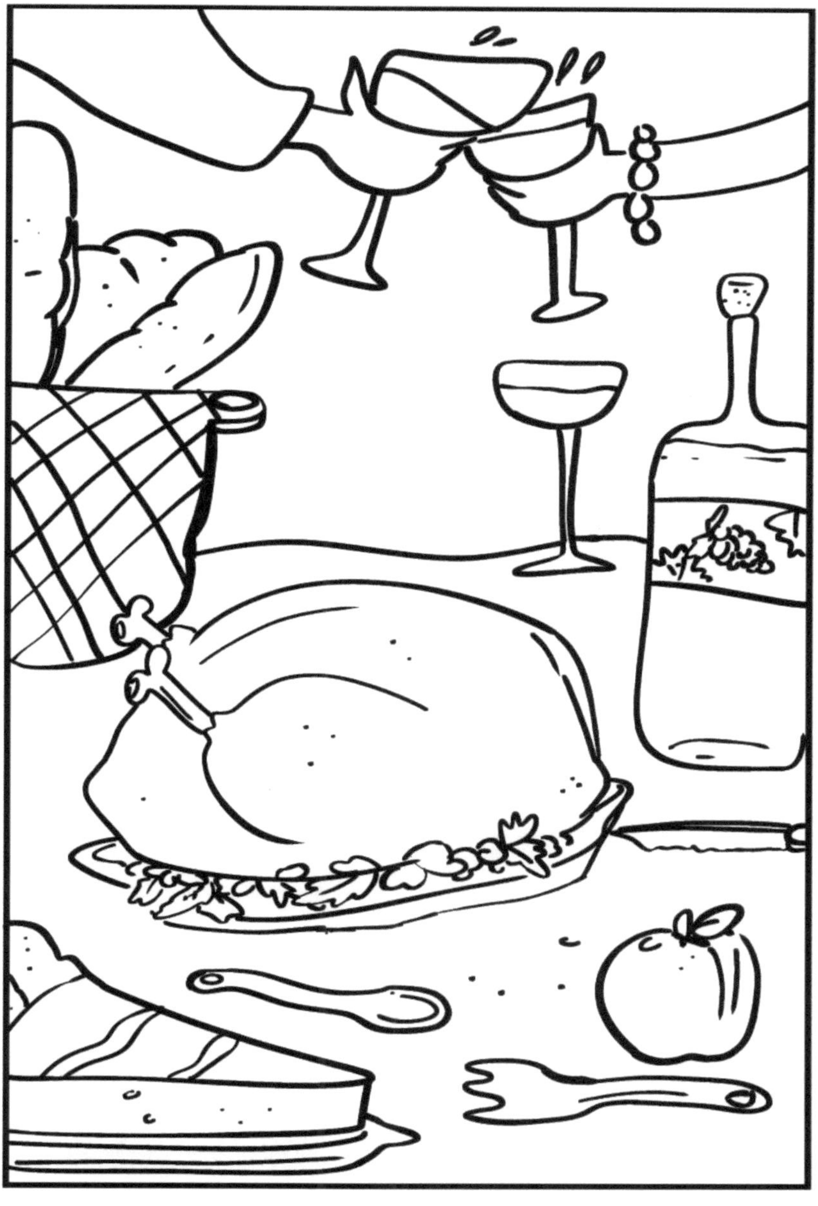

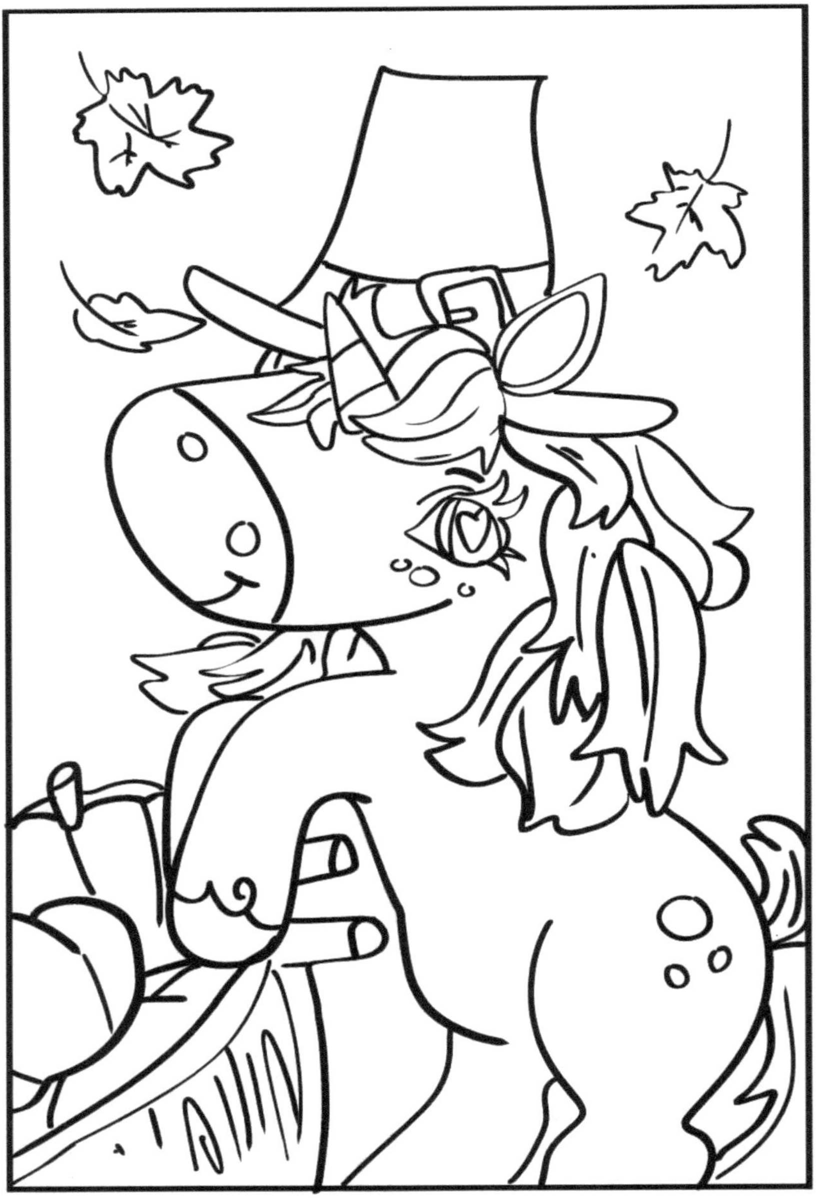

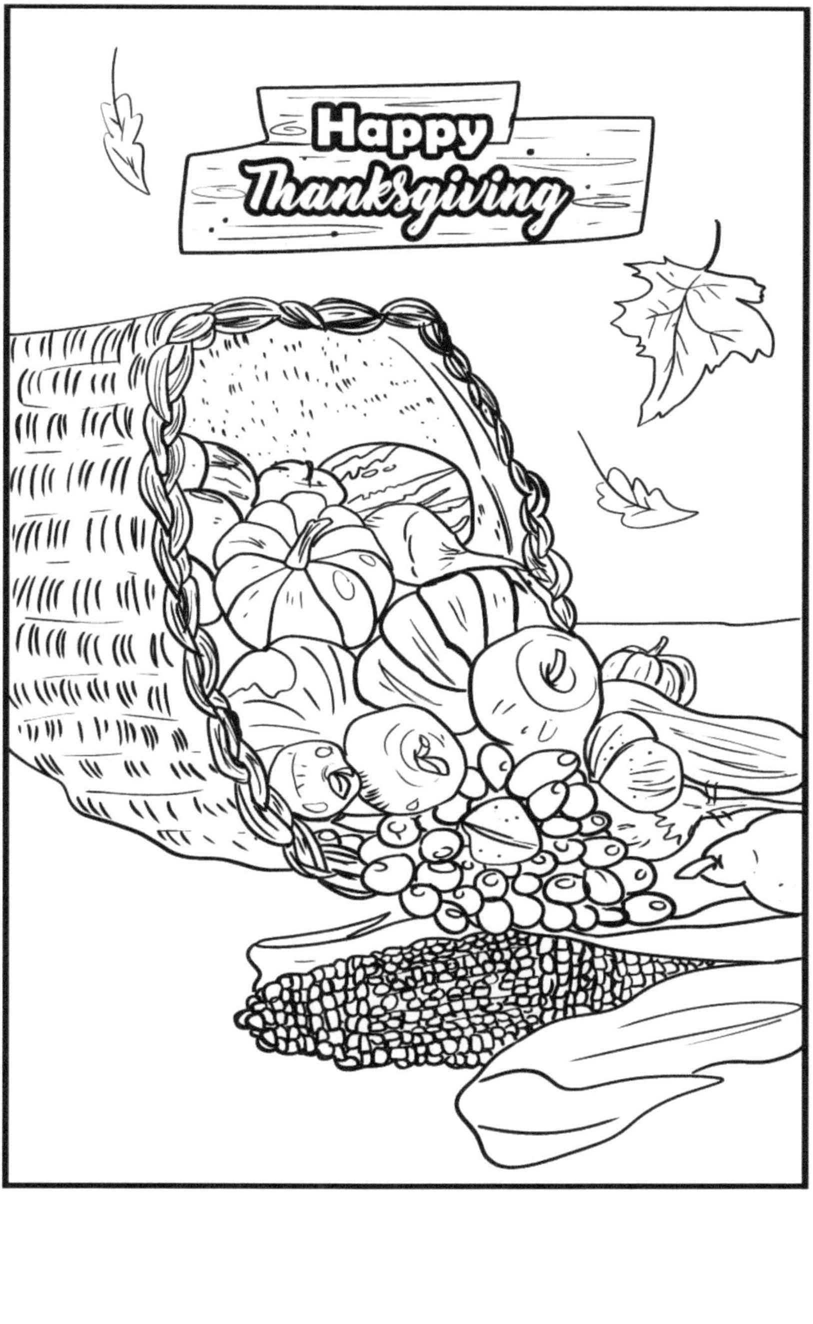
Happy
Thanksgiving

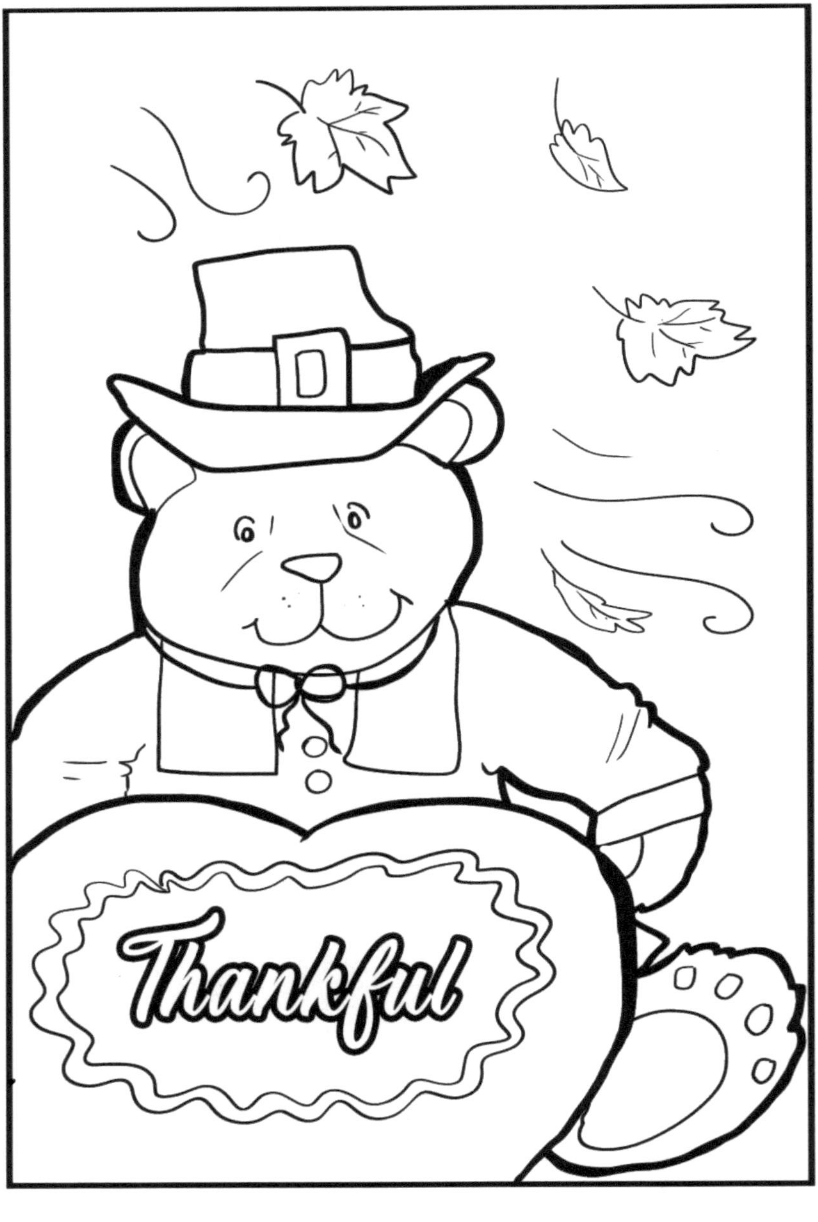
Thankful

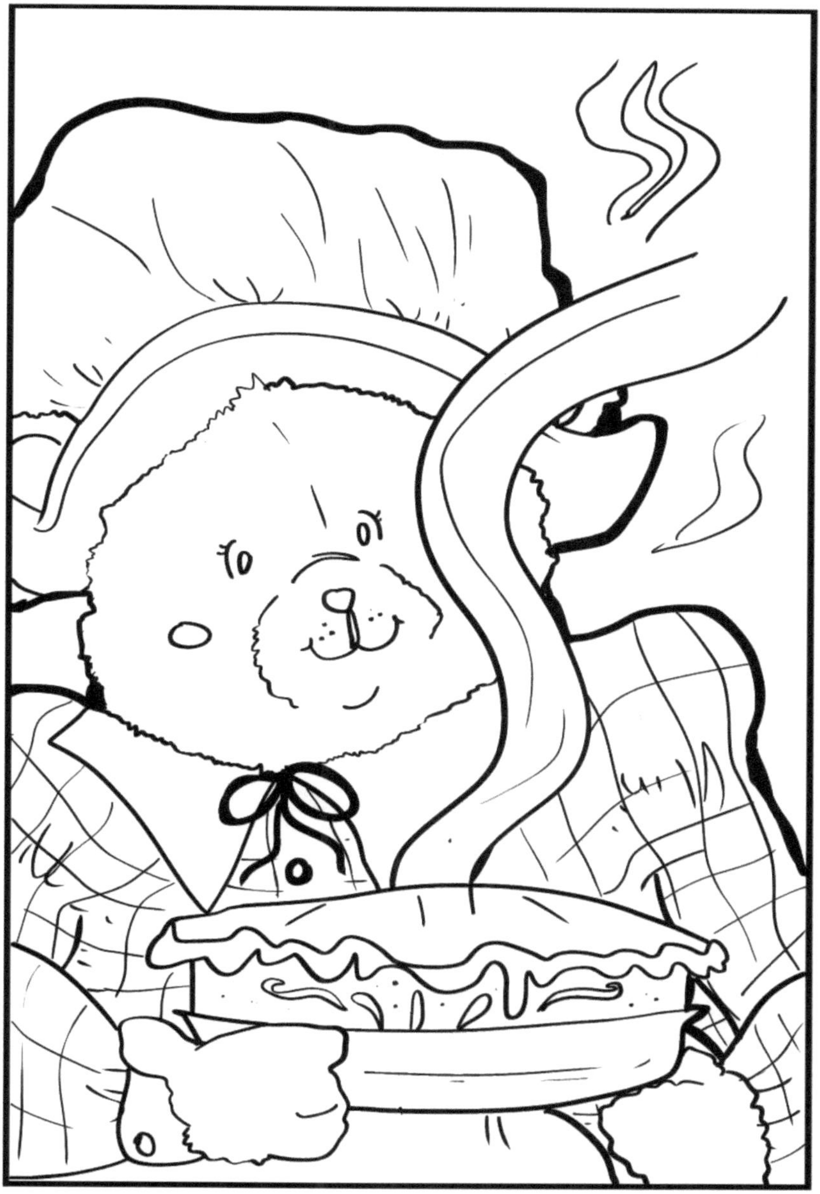

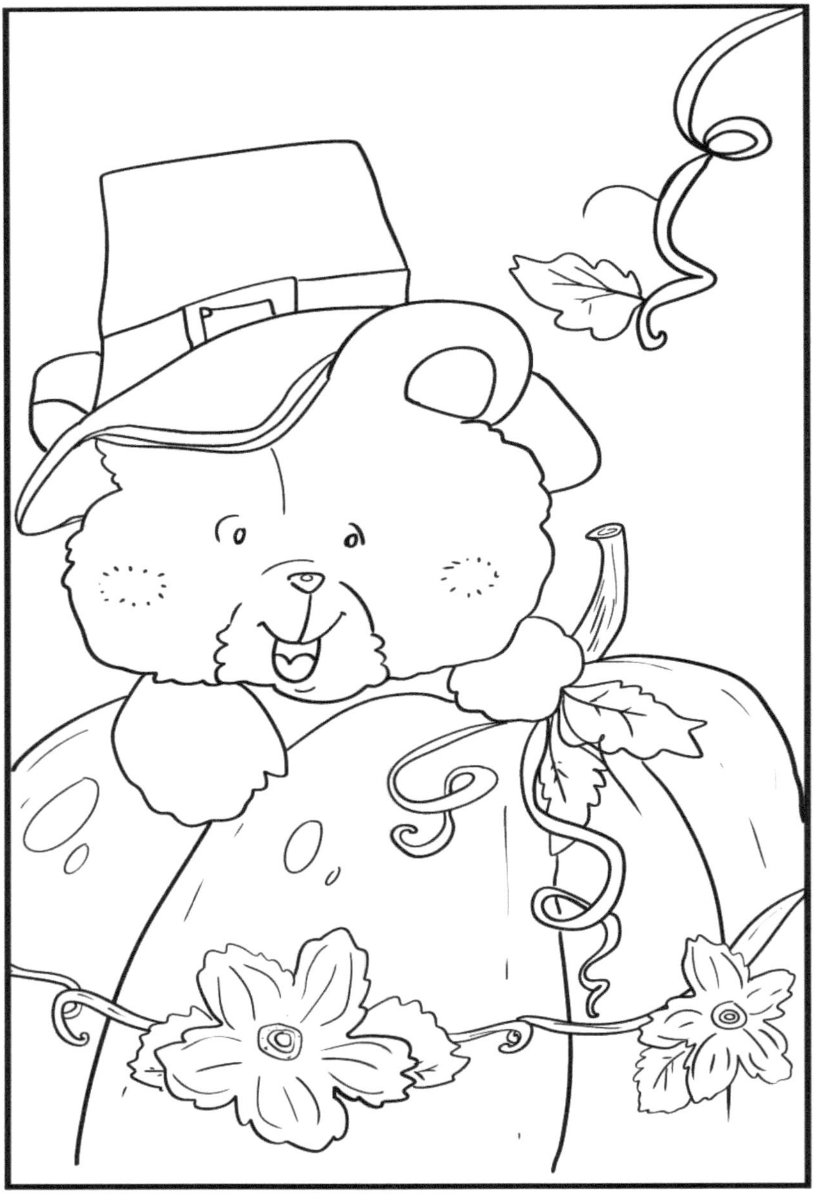

Happy
Thanksgiving

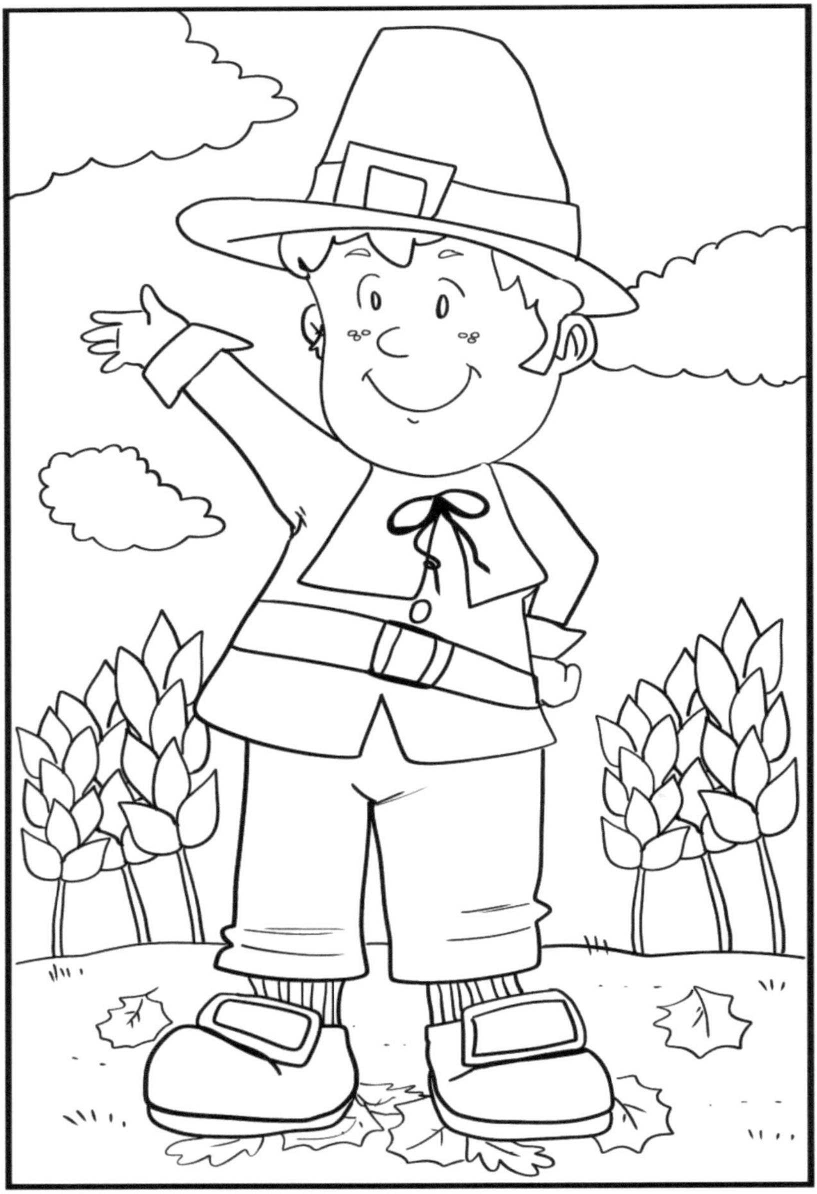

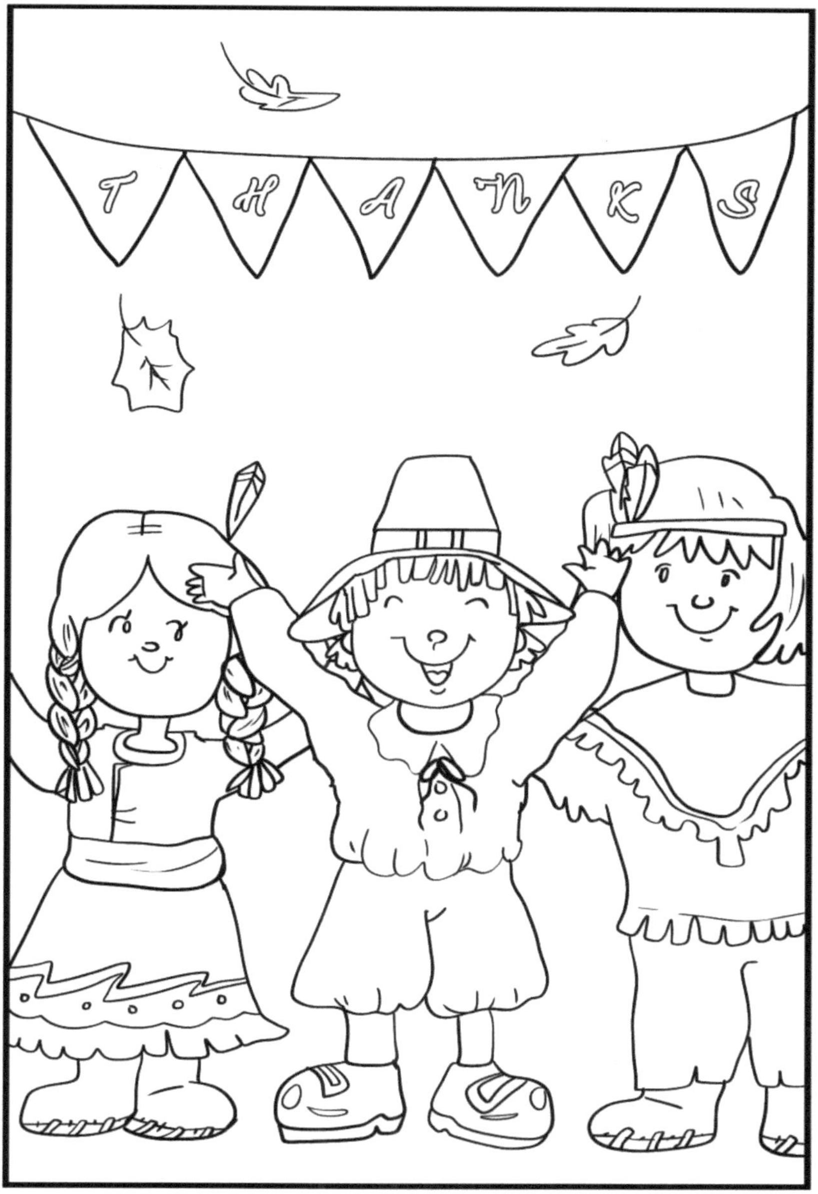
T H A N K S

Happy
Thanksgiving

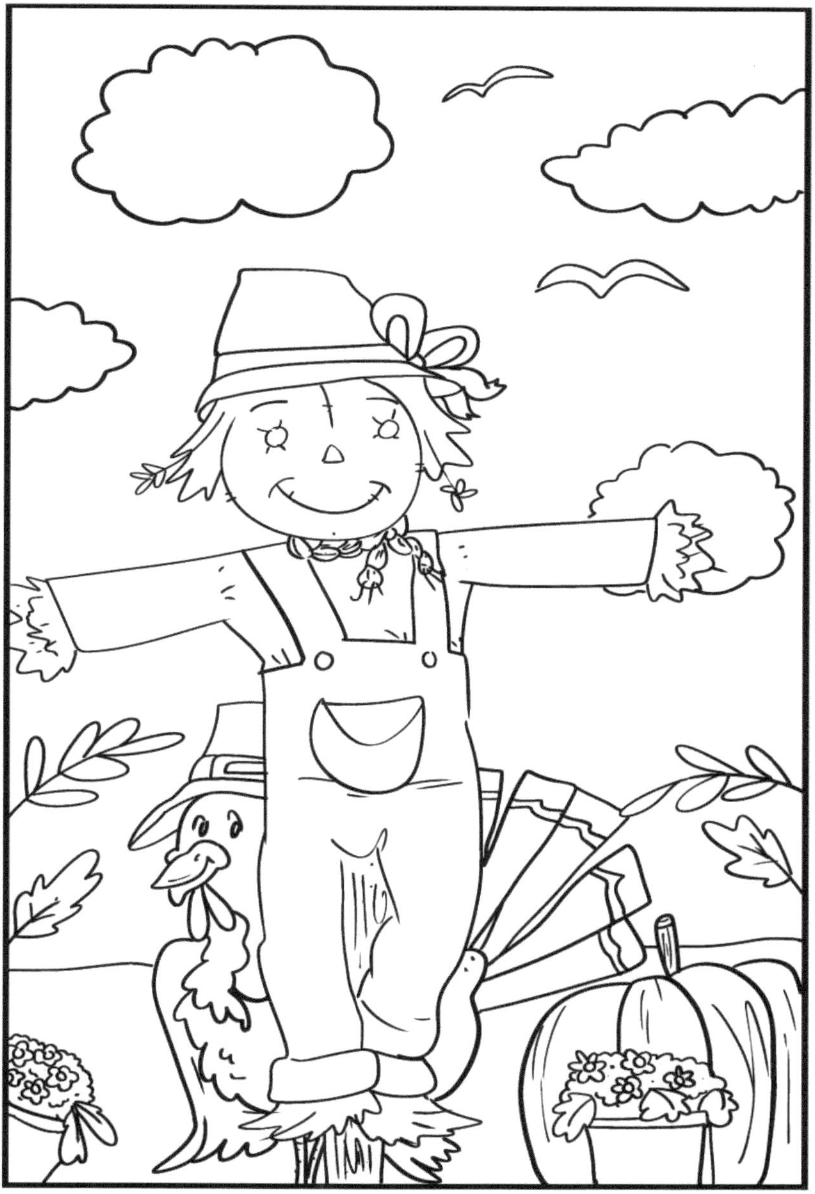

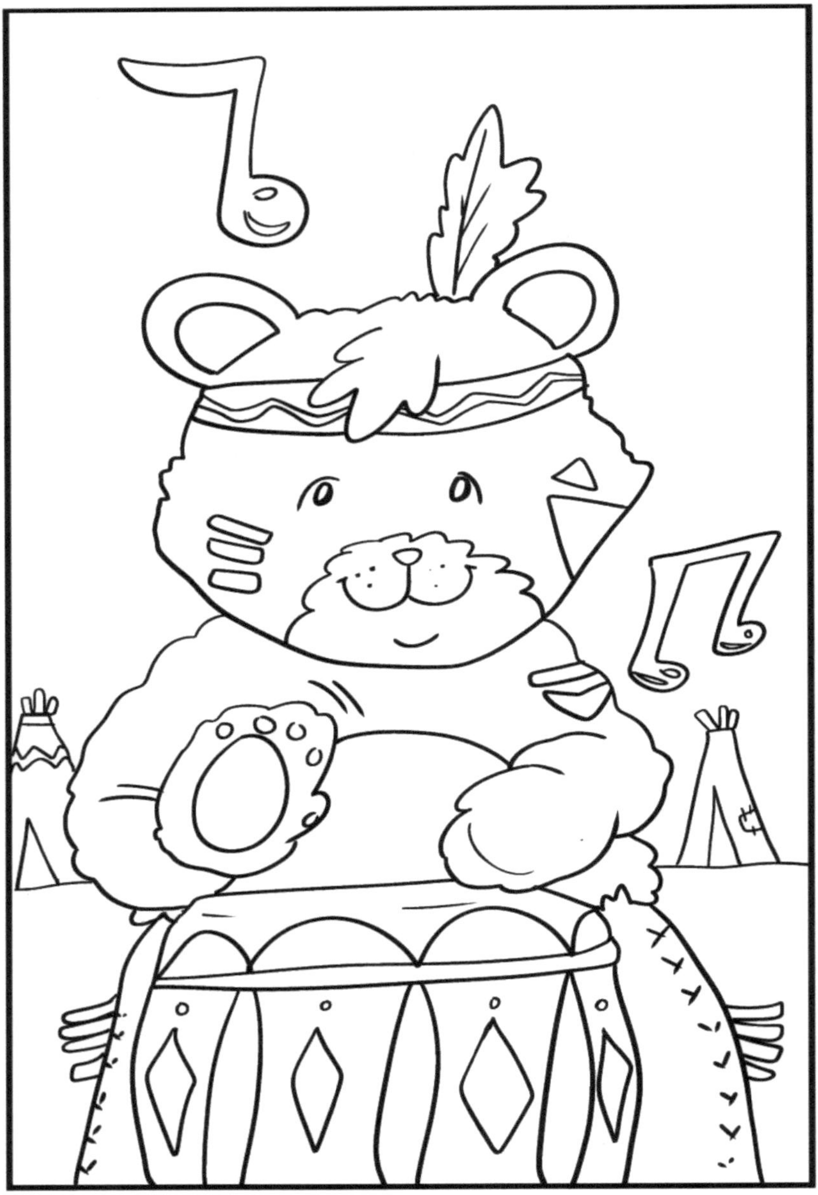

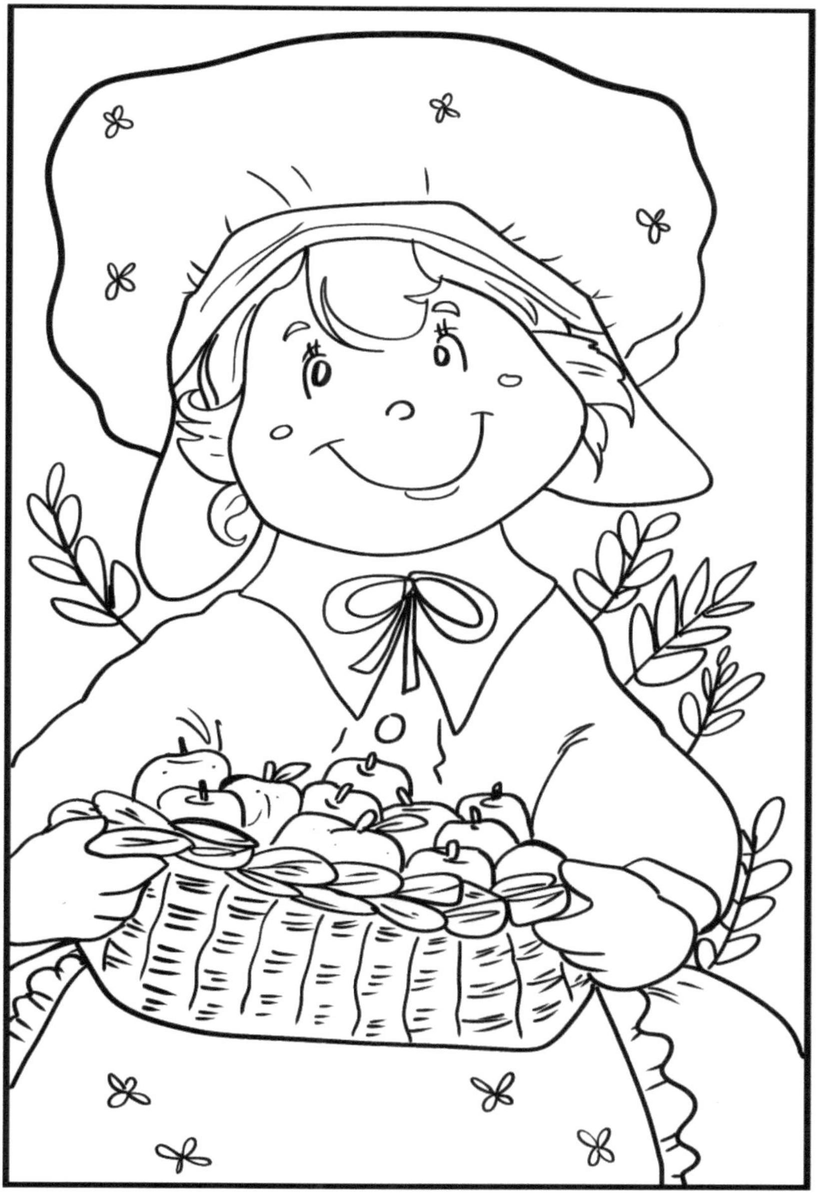

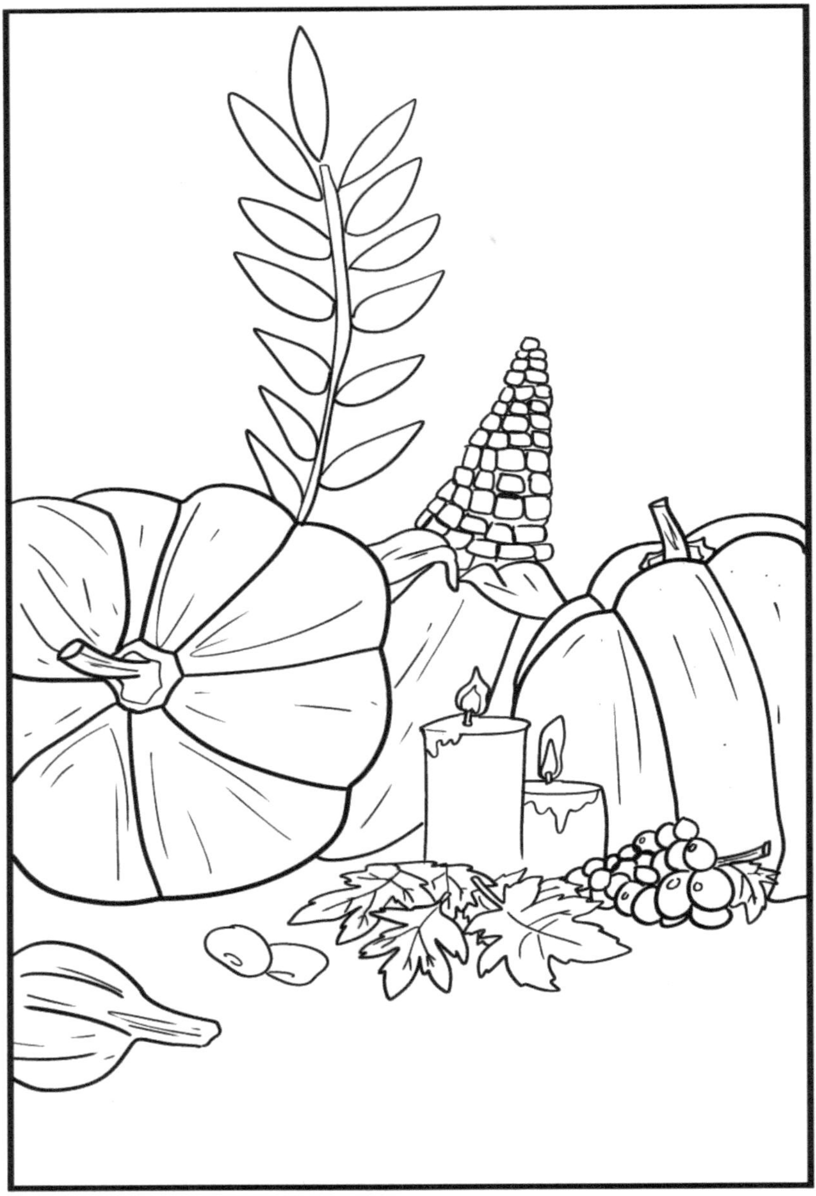

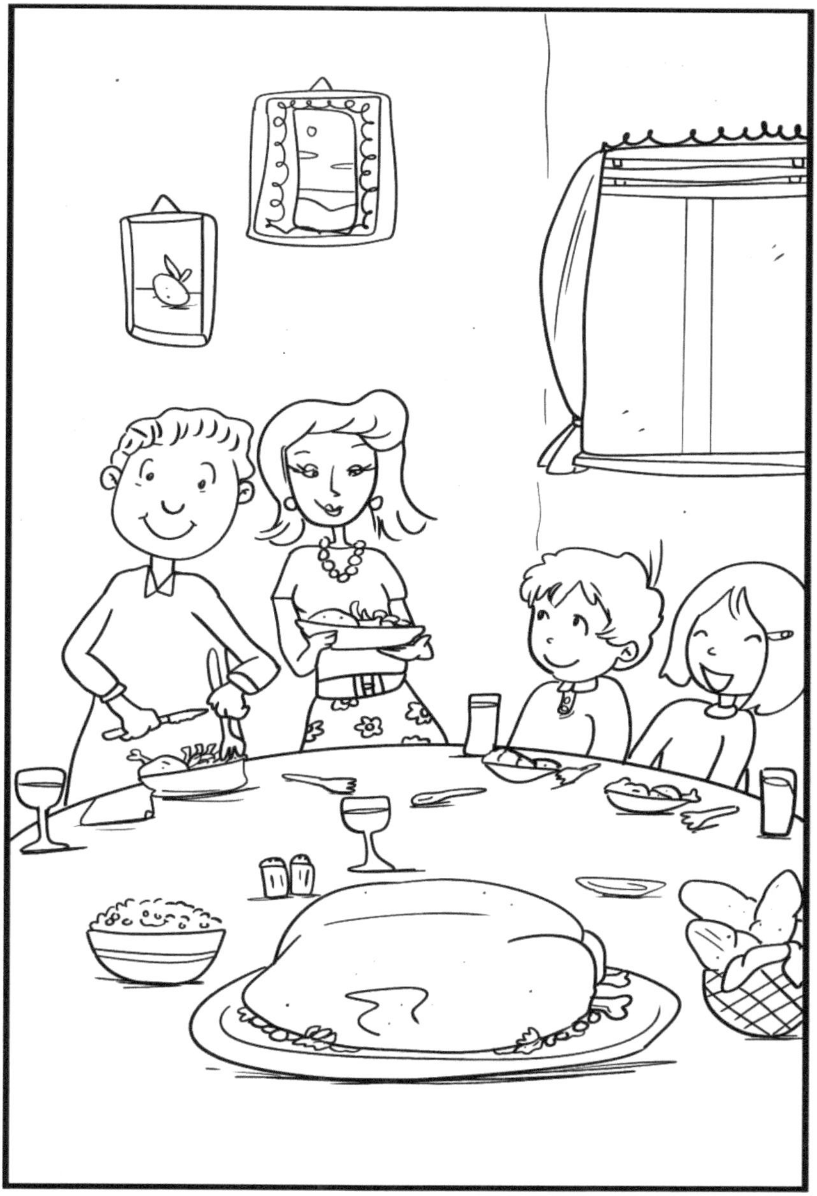

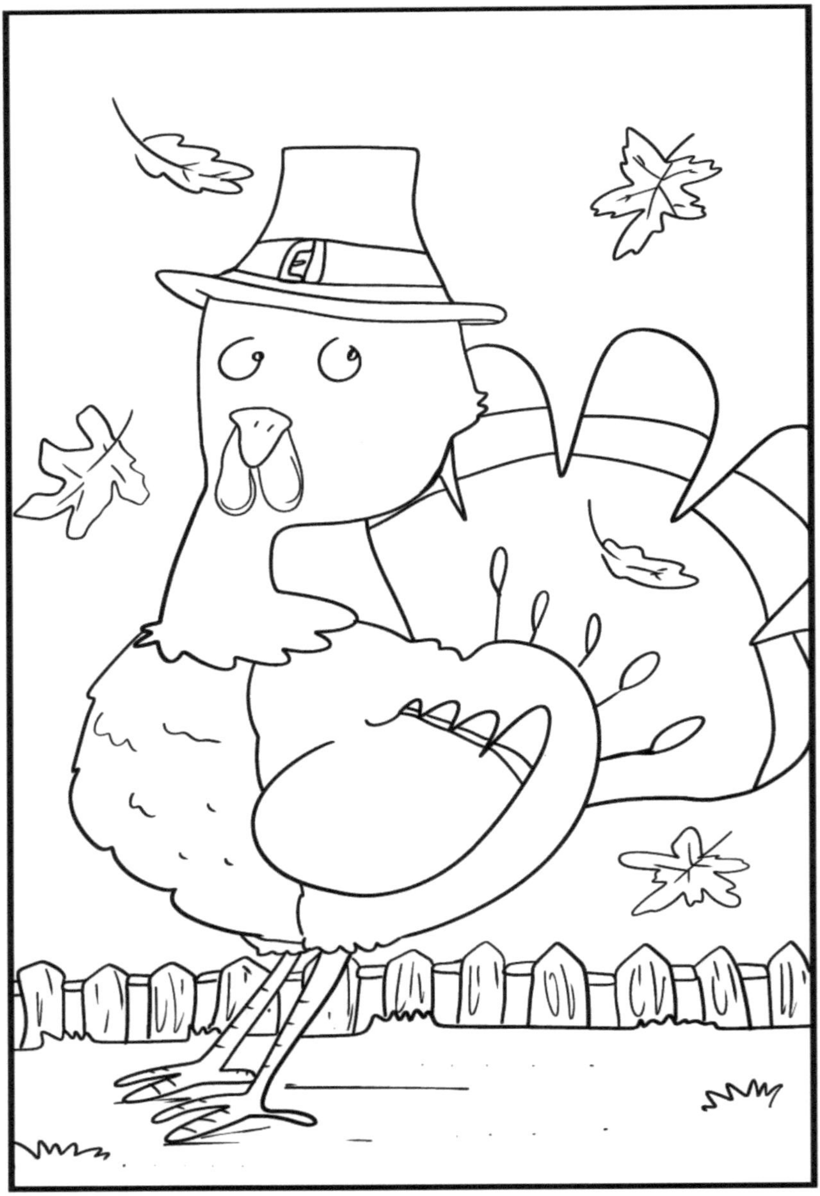

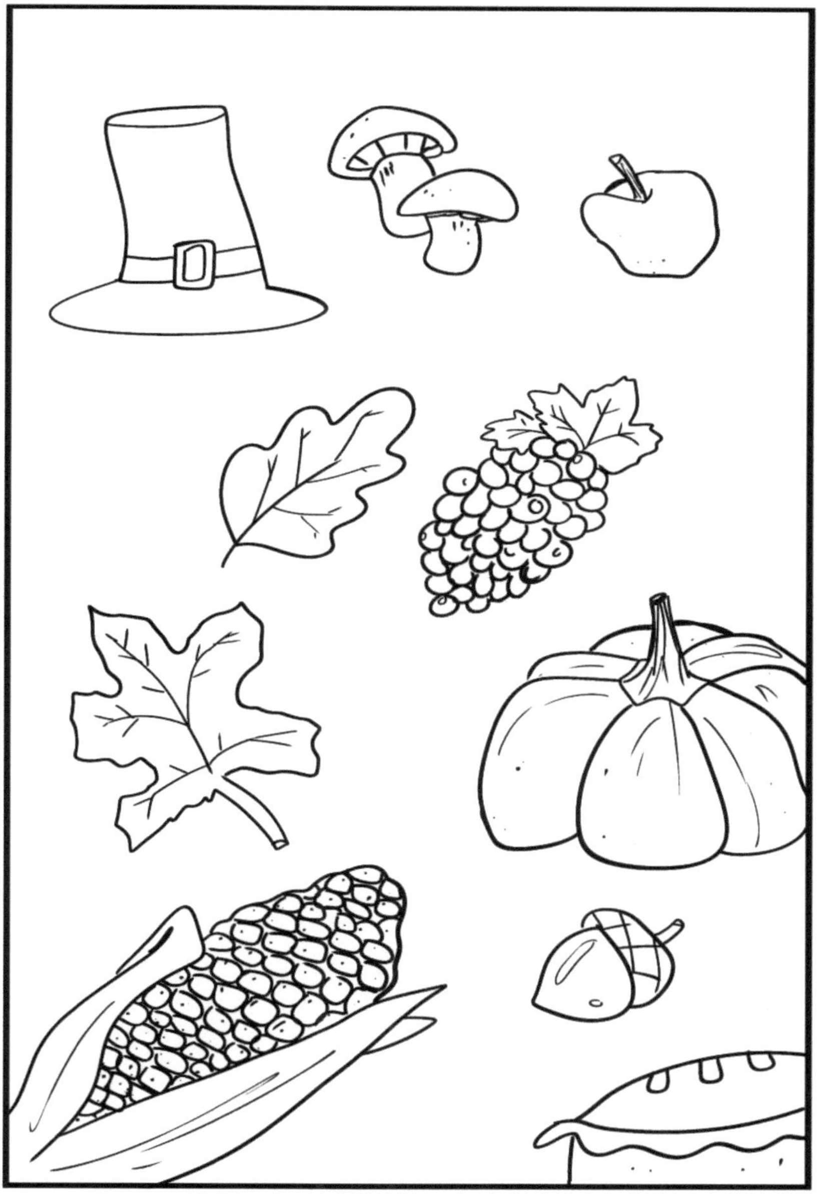

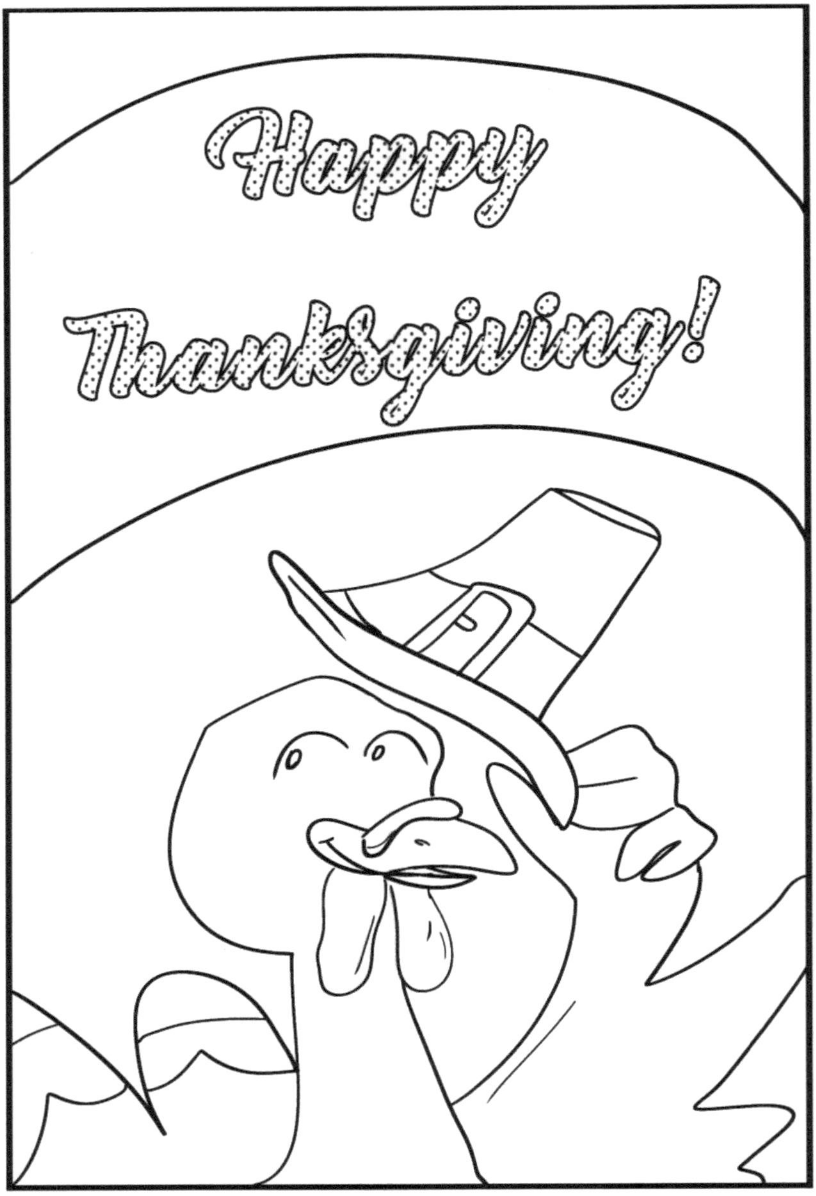
Happy
Thanksgiving!

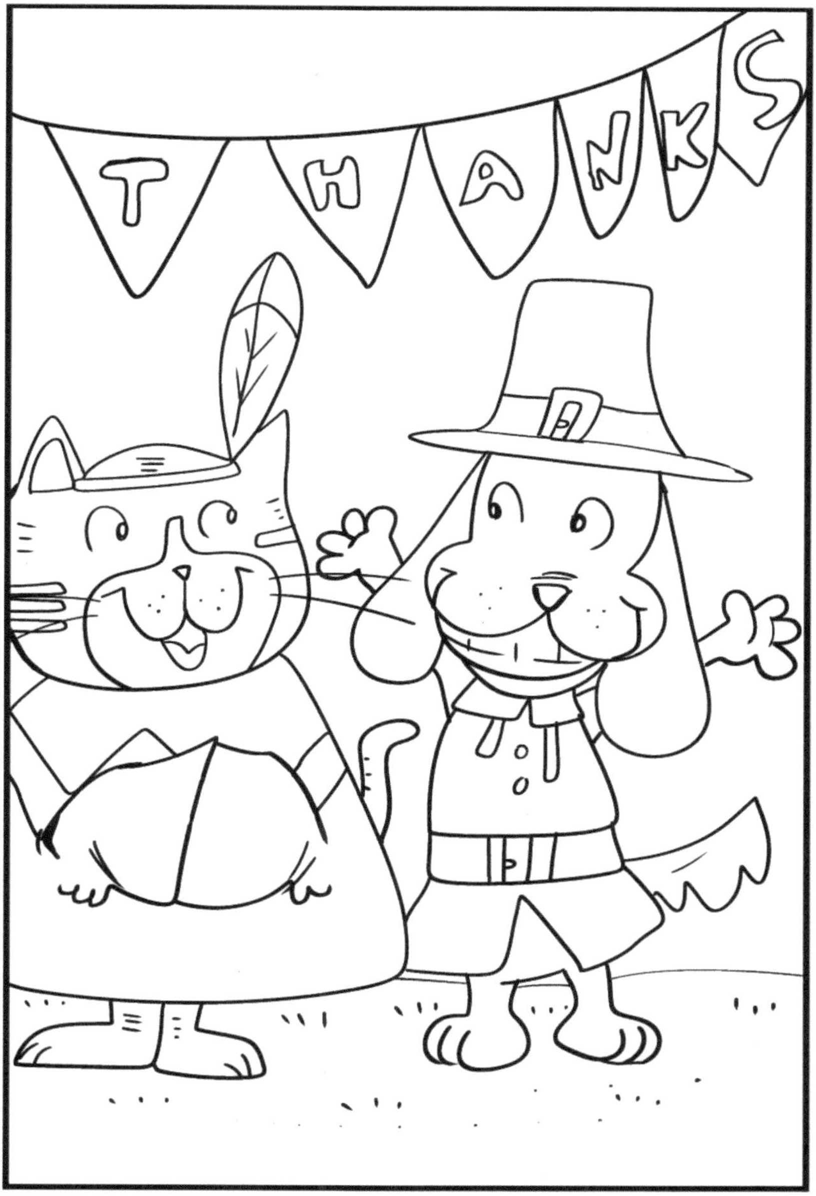
THANKS

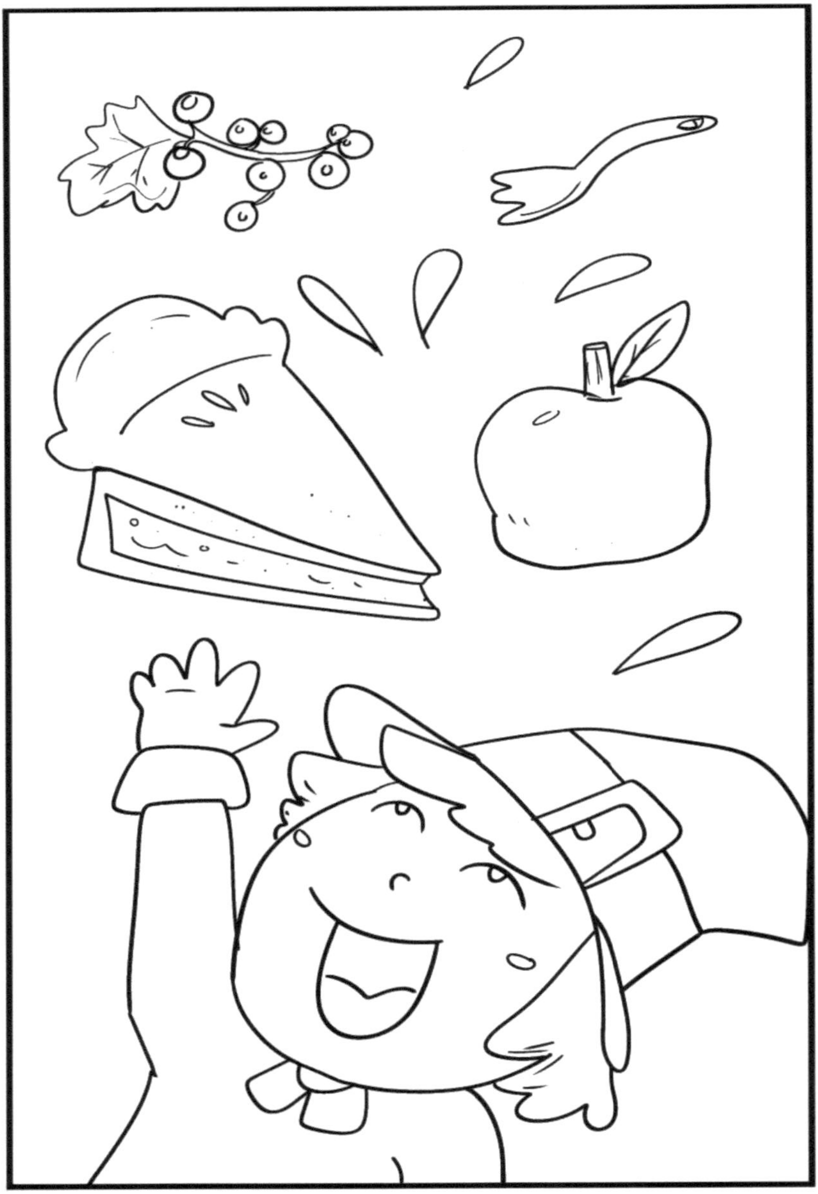

www.ingramcontent.com/pod-product-compliance
Lightning Source LLC
Chambersburg PA
CBHW041946240526
45473CB00033B/629
* 9 7 8 1 7 1 2 1 3 4 3 7 5 *